GW00857381

# The Bucket Book

## 100 things to do before you die

### Mickaël Nicotera

*MicNic* **Editions**

Text and illustrations : Mickaël Nicotera

# Contents

# How to use the Bucket Book ?

Highlight the things to do before you die
and then check it when they are done.

This book belongs to

..............................................................

# Travel

☐ **Climb up the Eiffel Tower**                    done on ........................

☐ **Walk on the Golden Gate bridge**               done on ........................

☐ **Visit New-York at Christmas time**             done on ........................

☐ **See the Grand Canyon**                         done on ........................

☐ **Have a picnic in Central Park**     done on .......................

☐ **See the Statue of Liberty**     done on .......................

☐ **See the Pyramids in Egypt**     done on .......................

☐ **Walk on the Great Wall of China**     done on .......................

☐ **See Niagara Falls**     done on .......................

☐ **Ride in a gondola in Venice**     done on .......................

☐ **Go on a cruise**     done on .......................

    done on .......................

☐ **Swim in Bora-Bora**

☐ **Climb Everest**                                done on .......................

☐ **Climb Kilimanjaro**                            done on .......................

☐ **Climb up the Empire State building**           done on .......................

☐ **Trek the Inca trail in Machu Picchu**          done on .......................

☐ **Add to the love lock bridge in Paris**         done on .......................

☐ **Walk on Hollywood Boulevard**                  done on .......................

☐ **Go sightseeing in Hollywood**                  done on .......................

☐ **Spend a night in Las Vegas**                   done on .......................

☐ **Visit Loch Ness in Scotland**                  done on .......................

Travel

☐ Drive on Route 66       done on ......................

☐ Spend a night in a cabin in the snow       done on ......................

☐ See Santa Claus in Lapland       done on ......................

☐ Visit a ghost town       done on ......................

☐ See the Great Barrier Reef       done on ......................

☐ See the moai of Easter Island       done on ......................

☐ Go on a dog sledding expedition in Alaska       done on ......................

☐ Visit Pompeii       done on ......................

☐ Hold up the Tower of Pisa       done on ......................

☐ Take a bath in the Ganges river       done on ......................

☐ **Visit Taj Mahal**                    done on ......................

☐ **Visit the White House**              done on ......................

☐ **Visit Tatooin in Tunisia**           done on ......................

☐ **Go to Dubai**                        done on ......................

☐ **Take the Orient Express**            done on ......................

☐ **See the Grand Opera house of Sydney**   done on ......................

☐ **Visit Uluru in Australia**           done on ......................

9

☐ Have one foot in the Northern Hemisphere and the other in the Southern Hemisphere at the equator line

done on ......................

☐ Float in the Dead Sea

done on ......................

☐ Drink Maple syrup in Canada

done on ......................

☐ Investigate in Roswell

done on ......................

☐ Go to Antarctica

done on ......................

☐ Visit an uninhabited island

done on ......................

☐ ..................................................

done on ......................

☐ ..................................................

done on ......................

☐ ..................................................

done on ......................

# Sports

☐ Go skydiving                done on ......................

☐ Do rafting                  done on ......................

☐ Complete a marathon        done on ......................

☐ Complete a half marathon    done on ......................

☐ Complete a triathlon         done on ......................

☐ Learn to surf                done on ......................

☐ Learn to skateboard         done on ......................

☐ **Learn to golf**                    done on ......................

☐ **Learn to ski**                     done on ......................

☐ **Go paintballing**                  done on ......................

☐ **Learn to ice skate**               done on ......................

☐ **Win any championship**             done on ......................

☐ **Go bungee jumping**                done on ......................

☐ **Walk over 4000 meters**      done on .........................

☐ **Learn a martial art**      done on .........................

☐ **Go scuba diving**      done on .........................

☐ **Attend an NBA game**      done on .........................

☐ **Attend a World Cup game**      done on .........................

☐ **Experience zero gravity**      done on .........................

☐ **Go to the Olympics**      done on .........................

☐ **Go zip lining**      done on .........................

☐ **Go parachuting**      done on .........................

☐ **Go bobsleighing**　　　　done on ......................

☐ **Go base jumping**　　　　done on ......................

☐ **Solve a Rubix-cube**　　　done on ......................

☐ **Catch a marlin**　　　　　done on ......................

☐ **Be able to do the splits**　done on ......................

☐ ................................................　done on ......................

☐ ................................................　done on ......................

☐ ................................................　done on ......................

# Transport

☐ **Travel by plane**            done on .......................

☐ **Fly first class**            done on .......................

☐ **Fly in a helicopter**            done on .......................

☐ **Fly a hot air balloon**            done on .......................

☐ **Travel by limo**       done on ........................

☐ **Take a submarine ride**       done on ........................

☐ **Ride an elephant**       done on ........................

☐ **Ride a camel**       done on ........................

☐ **Travel by seaplane**       done on ........................

☐ **Go parasailing**       done on ........................

☐ **Ride a jet ski**       done on ........................

☐ **Learn to fly**        done on ......................

☐ **Drive my favorite car : .....................**    done on ......................

☐ **Travel by hovercraft**       done on ......................

☐ ................................................................    done on ......................

☐ ................................................................    done on ......................

☐ ................................................................    done on ......................

17

# Nature

☐    **Sleep under the stars**        done on ......................

☐    **Milk a cow**        done on ......................

☐    **Find a four leaf clover**        done on ......................

☐    **Watch an eclipse**        done on ......................

☐    **Watch a meteor shower**        done on ......................

☐    **Watch a comet**        done on ......................

☐ **See an erupting volcano**  done on ........................

☐ **See a tornado**  done on ........................

☐ **Walk in a desert**  done on ........................

☐ **Walk in a rainforest**  done on ........................

☐ **Shower in a waterfall**  done on ........................

☐ **Watch whales**                          done on .....................

☐ **Swim with dolphins**                     done on .....................

☐ **Swim with sharks**                       done on .....................

☐ **Sea a Great White Shark up close**       done on .....................

☐ **Plant a tree**                           done on .....................

☐    **Go on safari**              done on ......................

☐    **Sleep in a tree house**          done on ......................

☐    **Swim in a hot spring**           done on ......................

☐    **See a wild orca**               done on ......................

☐    **See Northern Lights**           done on ......................

☐    **Gallop a horse along a beach**     done on ......................

☐    **See geyser erupt**             done on ......................

☐ Take pictures of 100 species of

......................................

done on ......................

☐ See another galaxy

done on ......................

☐ See an upside down rainbow

done on ......................

☐ See the green flash

done on ......................

☐ Walk on a glacier

done on ......................

☐ Watch a chunk of ice that breaks off a glacier and falls into water

done on ......................

☐ Wear a snake around my neck

done on ......................

☐ See a wild anaconda

done on ......................

☐ **Catch a wild piranha**                    done on .......................

☐ **Experience an earthquake**                done on .......................

☐ **See a carnivorous plant in Thailand**    done on .......................

☐ **See a Komodo dragon**                     done on .......................

☐ **See a platypus**                          done on .......................

☐ **Watch turtles hatch and run for the ocean**    done on .......................

☐ **See a wild jaguar**                       done on .......................

☐ **Pet a koala**                             done on .......................

☐ **Name a star**       done on .......................

☐ **Build a snowman**       done on .......................

☐ **Find a gem**       done on .......................

☐ **Find a meteorite**       done on .......................

☐ **Find a treasure**       done on .......................

☐ **Pick morels**       done on .......................

☐ **Pick horns of plenty (mushrooms)**       done on .......................

☐ ............................................................ done on ........................

☐ ............................................................ done on ........................

☐ ............................................................ done on ........................

# Delirium

☐ **Ride a roller coaster**        done on ........................

☐ **Go to a music festival**        done on ........................

☐ **Survive a haunted house**        done on ........................

☐ **Hunt a ghost**        done on ........................

☐ **Enjoy a feria**        done on ........................

☐ **Throw tomatoes at La Tomatina**        done on ........................

☐ Ride a big slide           done on ..........................

☐ Dance in the rain         done on ..........................

☐ Go skinny dipping         done on ..........................

☐ Go to a nude beach        done on ..........................

☐ Be part of a flash mob     done on ..........................

☐ Go to an oxygen bar       done on ..........................

☐ Own a poolroom          done on ..........................

☐ Own a pinball table       done on ..........................

Delirium

☐ **Go to San Diego Comic Con**       done on ........................

☐ **Stay awake for at least 24 hours**       done on ........................

☐ **Get hypnotized**       done on ........................

☐ **Own Chucky doll**       done on ........................

☐ **Wear a miniskirt**       done on ........................

☐ **Go into space**       done on ........................

☐ **Sleep in a castle**       done on ........................

☐ **Beat a Guinness World Record**       done on ........................

☐ **Escape from a room game**       done on ........................

☐ **Complete a game (........................)**       done on ........................

☐ **Attend a rocket launch**          done on ......................

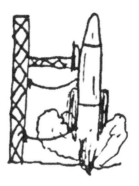

☐ **Meet an extraterrestrial**          done on .......................

☐ ............................................................          done on ......................

☐ ............................................................          done on .......................

☐ ............................................................          done on ......................

# Art

☐ **See Mona Lisa by Da Vinci**       done on ........................

☐ **Carve a pumpkin**       done on ........................

☐ **See a ballet**       done on ........................

☐ **Play on a stage**       done on ........................

☐ **Act in a movie**       done on ........................

☐ **Do yoga**       done on ........................

☐ **Read 100 books**                    done on ......................

☐ **Learn a new language**              done on ......................

☐ **Visit the Sistine Chapel**          done on ......................

☐ **Visit the tomb of ........................**   done on ......................

☐ **Visit the house of ........................**  done on ......................

☐ **Learn sign language**               done on ......................

☐ **Learn to juggle**                   done on ......................

☐ **Learn how to play ........................**   done on ......................

☐ **Draw a picture**                                         done on ......................

☐ **See .............................. in concert**          done on ......................

☐ **Meet my favorite star .......................**          done on ......................

☐ **Visit the Wizarding World of Harry Potter**             done on ......................

☐ **Visit the hobbit huts in New-Zealand**                  done on ......................

☐ **Go to a drive in movie theatre**                        done on ......................

☐ **Go to the filming location of**                         done on ......................
**........................................................**

☐ **Own 500 blurays**                                        done on ......................

# Watch every episode of

☐

.......................................................     done on ......................

☐     .......................................................     done on ......................

☐     .......................................................     done on ......................

☐     .......................................................     done on ......................

# Food

☐ **Eat caviar**                    done on .......................

☐ **Eat a burger in the USA**       done on .......................

☐ **Eat snails**                    done on .......................

☐ **Eat a raw oyster**              done on .......................

☐ **Eat pasta in Italy**            done on .......................

Food

☐ **Eat scorpions**                      done on ......................

☐ **Eat spiders**                        done on ......................

☐ **Eat frog legs**                      done on ......................

☐ **Eat insects**                        done on ......................

☐ **Eat caiman**                         done on ......................

☐ **Eat kangaroo**                       done on ......................

☐ **Eat snake**                          done on ......................

☐ **Drink overpriced wine**              done on ......................

Food

☐ **Have a brunch** done on .....................

☐ **Eat a very hot spice** done on .....................

☐ **Eat at a Michelin Star restaurant** done on .....................

☐ **Dine in the dark** done on .....................

☐ **Drink a delicious cocktail made with fresh fruits** done on .....................

☐ **Make my own jam** done on .....................

☐ **Make my own wine** done on .....................

☐ **Make my own ice cream** done on .....................

36

☐ **Bake my own bread**       done on ........................

☐ **Brew my own beer**       done on ........................

☐ ...............................................................       done on ........................

☐ ...............................................................       done on ........................

☐ ...............................................................       done on ........................

# Do it yourself

☐ **Build the (log) cabin of my dreams**     done on .......................

☐ **Build the house of my dreams**     done on .......................

☐ **Build an igloo**     done on .......................

☐ **Write a book**     done on .......................

☐  Send a message in a bottle          done on ......................

☐  Start a blog          done on ......................

☐  Own a fantastic collection of          done on ......................
...................................................

☐  Make my own jewelry          done on ......................

☐  Learn to sew          done on ......................

☐  Take a pottery class          done on ......................

☐  Knit a clothes          done on ......................

☐  Refurbish an old car          done on ......................

☐  Refurbish an old house          done on ......................

☐ **Trace my family tree**                    done on .......................

☐ **Write myself a letter, seal it and read it 10 years later**                    done on .......................

☐ .....................................................    done on .......................

☐ .....................................................    done on .......................

☐ .....................................................    done on .......................

# Life

☐ **Save a life**        done on .......................

☐ **Donate blood**        done on .......................

☐ **Meet the person of my life**        done on .......................

☐ **Get married**        done on .......................

☐ **Have children**        done on .......................

☐ **Adopt a child**        done on .......................

☐ **Adopt a pet**       done on ......................

☐ **Quit smoking**       done on ......................

☐ **Own my own business**       done on ......................

☐ **Get tattooed**       done on ......................

☐ **Open a B&B**       done on ......................

☐ **Get my driver's license**       done on ......................

☐ **Graduate from high school**       done on ......................

☐ **Go to college**       done on ......................

☐ **Graduate from university**       done on ......................

☐ Become a vegetarian                          done on ......................

☐ An entire week without phone, Internet or any screens       done on ......................

☐ Help with charity                         done on ......................

☐ Forgive ...........................................   done on ......................

☐ Be on TV                               done on ......................

☐ Hear my voice played on the radio   done on ......................

☐ Give a lecture                        done on ......................

☐ Move abroad to ...............................

for ............. years                done on ......................

☐ Dye my hair .........................    done on ......................

☐ **Win the lottery** done on ......................

☐ **Uncover the secret of the universe** done on ......................

☐ ............................................................ done on ......................

☐ ............................................................ done on ......................

☐ ............................................................ done on ......................

*Printed by Lulu.com*
February 2016
ISBN : 978-1-326-55129-2

Printed in Great Britain
by Amazon

73112578R00031